Incredible Girls & Amazing Women

Tales of astounding bravery & astonishing achievements

(and often, a bit of both).

Dedication

This book is for my own incredible girl, Millie, my son, Dylan and of course Dave, my (ever-patient) husband. Our cat will get his own dedication in the sequel.

Contents

Introduction

Bibliography & Further Reading

Introduction (probably for the grown-ups)

I started writing this book several years ago, when my daughter was only six years old. I was incredibly frustrated by the lack of female role models. So many women and girls who had achieved amazing things were hidden in history, or just not as prominent as women who have become famous for doing not very much (and certainly not much to be proud of).

This is not just a book for girls, this is a book for everyone who wants their children to understand the important role girls and women have played in shaping the world today.

Through researching this book, I came to understand a few things about what made these people successful. Some were (and are) incredibly intelligent, some incredibly beautiful and some were very rich. However, all of them faced a huge challenge, and armed with a strong sense of self-worth and determination, they achieved astonishing things. If we can all help our girls to grow up with this self-belief, we will make a positive difference to the next generation and the world.

Some of these stories include themes that can be very difficult but important to discuss with children. I hope you can forgive me where I have tempered and simplified these facts. This is in the hope that these stories can be shared as widely as possible. Please also use this book to pick and choose stories that you think will resonate with your children – there may be some stories that may be too tricky to discuss just ahead of bed time!

We are living in very uncertain times. Times where despite all the progress the world has made – it is still difficult to be a strong girl or a strong woman. I have written this book to help our children understand the contribution of girls and women of all ages, from different religions, countries and backgrounds to making an incredible, positive difference to the world.

To honour this personal commitment, I am donating 10% of all profits from this book to charities that support girls and women across the world. One of the UK charities I'm delighted to be supporting is Girlguiding. It builds girls' confidence and raises their aspirations.

I hope you like it.

Jenni

Chapter 1: Malala

Far, far away in a country called Pakistan is a beautiful place called the Swat Valley. A crystal clear stream runs through the valley from the distant purple mountains and the grass is lush. Fragrant figs and pomegranates hang from the trees like jewels and the meadows are full of the contented yet busy hum of insects. Many years ago, when this story begins, many villages were dotted across this valley. People travelled between them, selling their wares, sharing news and living in harmony. Although they were poor, and sometimes challenged by bad weather and illness - their lives were simple and full.

By chance one day, a young man visited his family in the next door village and saw from afar a beautiful girl. He fell deeply in love with her. Although the young man was not classically handsome, but because he was an amazing storyteller and expressed himself beautifully through poetry, the girl fell madly in love with him. With the blessing of their families, they soon married and had a baby girl. But this isn't the end of the story, this is only the beginning!

In this land, for many different reasons, people thought that having a baby girl wasn't good news. Most people really wanted to have sons, so that they would have someone to work the farms and support their family in the future. Traditionally, girls were not allowed to go to school, and had to stay at home until they were ready to have marriages arranged for them. Women and girls were seen as less important than boys and men.

When the little girl was born, her mother and father were overcome with love for their beautiful daughter. They called her Malala, after a famous poet and warrior woman. The family lived happily in the Swat Valley and Malala's father set up a school in the village. It wasn't a school as you would know it. It was very simple, with a dusty floor, chalkboards and books that were old and handed down from class to class.

Even when Malala was a little baby, she used to accompany her father to the school. School was a busy place, full of love and energy. She enjoyed the attention the pupils and teachers gave her, and whiled away hours sitting in the classrooms listening in to pupils' lessons. Her love of education and learning started from an early age.

Around the time of Malala's tenth birthday, new, strange men came to the valley. They talked of war and spread fear between the people. They threatened the villagers with cruel punishments if they did not obey their commands. First, they demanded that girls should not mix with boys. The school had no choice but to separate into two different schools. From then on, boys and girls were educated separately. Many other demands followed. The men tried to make girls stay at home, they tried to prevent girls from going to school and they demanded that girls must cover themselves up. Across the valley, village by village succumbed to the fear of the punishments if they disobeyed. Girls stopped going to school and schools were shut down.

Few people stood up to these men, as they were afraid of what would happen to their families and their livelihoods. Malala and her father both believed that every child had a right to an education and that girls should be allowed to go to school and learn to read and write and to study the things that you and I take for granted.

But it wasn't that simple.

Malala and her father decided to stand up to these men. Not by fighting and using guns, but by using words – the most powerful weapon of all. Malala started writing about her daily life and her school and publishing it online. Through the power of the internet, people all across the world started to read her blog and understand how difficult it was for the girls at her school to have a chance to learn without being threatened by people who disagreed with them. Soon, newspapers, radio and TV channels got to hear of Malala and the power of her words grew and grew. Because of her writing - her country's government started to pay attention to the difficulties that the people in her valley were facing from the armed men. She met with many important people, including the President of her country, governments from across the world, journalists and people who wanted to support the right for children to get an education.

Because she talked from the heart, and spoke simply, bravely and honestly about the difficulties that she faced - Malala's fame grew and grew. Sadly, so did the threats made against her by the band of men. They were angered that someone that they thought was 'just a girl' was getting so much attention. They did not like people protesting against their rules.

Just after Malala turned fifteen, something terrible happened. She was on her way to school, on the school bus that took her and her friends to class, when someone got on the bus. He asked 'Where is Malala?'. No one answered, but the man knew who he was looking for. He walked up to Malala and shot her.

Very few people survive being shot, especially so close up. But through what some might call good luck, a miracle, or an angel looking out for Malala – it was not her time to die. The gunshot wound was terrible, a bullet passed right through her skull and people thought she would not survive. She was taken by helicopter from her valley to the capital city of her country, where she had many operations. Then, she was flown out of her country into the UK for even more hospital treatment.

At this point, the whole world became Malala's family. People across the globe united, stood up and supported her. Just one girl, brave enough to stand up for what she believed in, became a heroine and a role model for the world.

Malala has recovered. What she has seen and experienced has changed her and her family. They have had to leave the country that they loved to make sure that they could be safe. But what she has done to stand up for children across the world having the right to be educated, has changed us all for the better.

In 2014, Malala won the Nobel Prize for Peace – one of the greatest prizes that can be awarded to anyone in the world. Her charity, The Malala Fund, wants to see a world where every girl can complete 12 years of safe, quality education and works hard to achieve this.

Twenty years ago, she was just a girl, in a valley far, far away, that nobody really ever thought of. Now she has countries and world leaders hearing her words and taking action and she is changing the lives of millions of girls for the better.

Chapter 2: Ada Lovelace

Two hundred years ago, Ada Lovelace was born to extraordinary parents. Her father, Lord Byron, was a world famous poet. Byron was incredibly handsome and charming and led a wild and daring life. It was said that any woman who saw him would fall desperately in love with him. He was the closest thing that the world had to a rock star!

Ada's mother, Annabella, was a very clever woman. However, she was the complete opposite of Lord Byron. Where Lord Byron loved spending money and living a crazy and glamorous life, she much preferred logic, order and keeping her money safe and sound. From the very moment they got together and throughout their marriage, they disagreed on pretty much everything.

Ada was only six weeks old when Annabella decided to leave Lord Byron for good. They were two completely different people, and she could not bear his crazy lifestyle any more. Byron's behaviour had been too much for Annabella's sensible ways. It was a cold January night in busy, smoky London and Annabella gathered up Ada and her belongings and stole out into the frosty evening. She returned as fast as she could to her family home and sadly, Ada would never see her father again.

Annabella lived in fear that Ada would turn out to be like Lord Byron and that she would love poetry and wild, extravagant living. She was so worried about this, that she never let Ada see a picture of Lord Byron until she was fully grown up. She also made sure that Ada, who had inherited her mother's talent for numbers and logical thinking, was taught a great deal about mathematics in a bid to keep her away from the poetry and words that her father so loved.

Despite Annabella's attempts to focus Ada's talents, she grew up to be a perfect mix of both her parents. She had an incredible mind. Ada was creative with a daring imagination, but amazing at maths and science. While other young ladies of the time bustled about in dresses and were taught just enough to be able to snare a good husband - Ada, with her determination and great brain, was considered to be quite remarkable.

It was the time of the Industrial Revolution. People were understanding more and more about the world around them. The more people learnt, the more they discovered and the more they discovered, the faster they created exciting new inventions. Steam engines, sewing machines, dynamite and the London Underground were just a few of the things that were invented. It may feel like this was a very long time ago, but it was in this time that Ada was to invent something that changed the world forever. Ada helped create the very first computer.

One of the most exciting things to do at this time, was to visit exhibitions showing the latest inventions. It was at one of these exhibitions where it all began. Ada met Charles Babbage, an inventor and scientist who was demonstrating his new machine, the 'Analytical Engine'. It was a huge clockwork machine, with cogs and levers that he believed would be capable of doing maths and 'thinking' without human help. If you are interested, it can be seen in London's Science

Museum today.

Ada was only eighteen years old, but she was completely mesmerised. Unlike many of the incredibly intelligent scientists who had seen the invention, she was able to imagine and understand the huge potential of creating a machine that could think for itself! Once finished, the machine would be able to carry out calculations by turning the question into a special code and then using the same code to answer it. The thinking machine would be able to carry out really difficult sums faster than a human (and make no mistakes!). This in turn would help the factories that were being built all across the world make their products even faster and better.

What excited Ada even more (and that no one else had thought of) was that anything could be turned into a code – words, music and even pictures. It became her life's mission to turn Charles' invention into a perfectly working machine. And, like all great inventors, she was obsessed.

She visited Charles Babbage as much as she could.

In those days, it was most irregular to have a young lady visiting people alone, but her mother soon understood that nothing would stop Ada from helping build the machine. She was incredibly determined.

Very soon, the 'Analytical Engine' was attracting interest from all across the world. One important scientist wrote a long essay in French about the potential of the machine. Ada set to work translating it for Charles, adding her own ideas in the margins. It was here that she wrote about her own ideas for machines that could perform thinking tasks. This is the very first time that someone had ever imagined computing as an important and new idea. Ada also understood that being a woman in this time, meant that her ideas would be cast aside as fanciful or silly, so whenever she wrote these ideas down – she gave them her initials, not her full name.

For many years, Ada's obsession with the machine continued. When Ada and Charles could not see each other in person, they communicated in long letters. In one of these letters, Ada suggested some ways in which she thought the machine could be improved and some mistakes that she had spotted in Charles' calculations. Unfortunately, he was to ignore her suggestions. However, her instructions were to be the first example of a computer programme (which you and I know as coding). Ada's passion and love for the machine and the possibilities it created, meant that she invented not just computing but coding too!

Sadly, the machine never worked in the ways that Ada believed possible. This was partly due to a lack of money to support the Analytical Engine and partly because Charles refused to pay attention to Ada's suggestions. We will never know what could have been achieved if Ada had been properly allowed to apply her amazing gifts of imagination and maths to the machine.

When she was in her thirties, Ada got very ill and sadly died, coincidentally at the same age as her father.

But Ada's story does not end there. About 90 years

later, a man called Alan Turing read her papers. Turing was to create a machine, partially based on the Analytical Engine, that was to begin what some people call the 'Age of Computing'. (What they mean by that is that without computers, modern life would be impossible and these days we need and use them for everything). Without Ada's vision – we cannot be certain that this would ever have happened.

Ada is now known as the 'Mother of Modern Computing' and recognised for her huge contribution to the world. Every year, scientists and inventors across the world celebrate her birthday and the achievements of women in science. It's the perfect day to say a huge thanks for making it possible for girls and women all over the world to invent, code and create even better computers.

Chapter 3: Hedy Lamarr

Hedy was an only child, born in Vienna, who spent a great deal of her time imagining and inventing things to save her from boredom. She grew up in a particularly difficult time. The first Great War had happened, where millions of people had lost their lives and now, new leaders were starting to come to power who were intent on causing more trouble and potentially another huge War.

By the time she was 16, Hedy had become a professional actress. This was not just because she was considered incredibly beautiful, but most importantly, because she was particularly determined to succeed. Once, when she badly wanted to win an acting role, she moved to a different city to win the part. Hedy wasn't obsessed with what people looked like on the outside, she believed that what people could achieve was most important. As she once said "Any girl can be glamorous. All you have to do is stand still and look stupid." After becoming famous across Europe for the movies that she had starred in, Hedy married Fritz Mandl, a rich and powerful man. He didn't particularly like his wife being the centre of attention, so he persuaded her to give up acting.

Fritz had become rich by selling weapons to different countries, and Hedy often was present when Fritz met important people to discuss these deals. It was these meetings that started a germ of an idea for Hedy, that over 40 years later would be the start of one of the most important inventions for the world as we know it!

After a few years of marriage, Hedy became very unhappy. Fritz was very suspicious and controlling. He liked to know where Hedy was and what she was doing all of the time. He listened in to her conversations and wouldn't even let her go swimming by herself! As you can imagine, Hedy wasn't comfortable being told what to do by her husband and being watched all the time. She came up with a plan to leave her husband for good and become a famous Hollywood star. It was a bold and brave idea that needed determination, planning and a great deal of cunning.

Hedy was going to use her acting skills for a very daring escape, which took several months of planning. She made friends with one of her maids that looked the most like her, called Laura. She practiced how Laura walked, how she talked and made sure that she could do a perfect impersonation of her.

One evening, she tricked Laura into drinking a sleeping potion and falling asleep. She placed Laura in Hedy's bed and covered her up so that only her hair was peeking out over the covers. Hedy's heart was beating fast and her stomach was more knotted than a climbing rope as she dressed up as Laura. Then she walked out of the house as calmly as possible, down the driveway (even waving goodbye to other maids) and escaping on the train to Paris and then across the English Channel to London. It was probably one of her most important acting roles. Hedy was finally free!

The next step was for Hedy to become a successful

Hollywood movie star. At a glamorous event in London, she met with a very famous and powerful film producer called Louis B Mayer. He could see that she had star quality and offered her a chance to become an actress in Hollywood. However, Louis offered her a very small salary. Where some people would have been grateful and jumped at the chance - Hedy was confident enough to believe she was worth more, and walked out of the meeting.

Again, Hedy had a cunning plan. She wanted to work with Louis B. Mayer, but she wanted to earn a more money. She booked herself on the same ship that was taking Louis and his wife back to America. It was a long journey and Hedy used it to the best of her ability. Through making friends with everyone and always looking glamorous, Hedy made sure that she was the most popular passenger on the ship. Louis could not help but notice that wherever Hedy went on the boat, she was the centre of attention! Within a few weeks, Hedy was offered a movie deal with lots more money. She was delighted.

Over the next few years, Hedy became a massive Hollywood star and was known as the most beautiful woman in the world. Her movies were some of the most popular of the time. However, these were troubled times. World War 2 had broken out, and because her home country of Austria had been invaded by the Nazis, she felt desperate to do what she could to help the Allies (the Americans and British and many other countries) fight and win the War.

Because she was so famous and glamorous, the Americans used Hedy to attend fundraising events to support the War effort. Hedy was happy to help out, but was frustrated that she hadn't had the chance to use her brain. She wanted to do more!

Hedy loved inventing. She had created a special den in her glorious mansion where she spent her spare time creating new products and solutions to everyday problems. Her ideas included a new kind of traffic light, a special contraption to dispose of used tissues and, like a real life Willy Wonka, she invented a magic cube that would turn into a drink like Coca Cola when you added water. Sadly, these never became successful inventions, but one day, when she was thinking up ways to defeat the enemies - she came up with an incredible idea.

There had been a terrible incident, where a German torpedo (which is a rocket which goes through the water) had hit a boat and lots of innocent people had died. Hedy, like the rest of the world, was really upset by this news. Torpedoes are directed to their target by a remote control. If you've ever played with a remote control toy, you might know that the toy and the control both speak to each other on the same frequency or channel. If someone wanted to stop you controlling the toy - all they would have to do would be to jam (or stop) that channel.

Hedy wanted to make sure that the Allies' torpedoes always hit their target and to stop the enemies' torpedoes from hitting innocent people. So she set to work with one of her friends, a composer called George Antheil.

Hedy's big idea was to create a way to communicate to the object on not just one channel, but to switch channels all the time. This would confuse the enemies and keep control of the object. Her 'frequency hopping' idea was a bold and daring. The invention had so much potential that Hedy and George applied for a patent. (A patent is a way to protect your idea, so that if anyone copies it or uses it, you are still considered the owner and have control over it.)

George and Hedy successfully gained a patent for this idea in 1942. Hedy was worried that people would not take it seriously if she was named on the patent, and that it would draw attention to the invention. As a result, Hedy used her old married name to conceal her identity. After the patent was filed, news of her idea reached the American Navy. They were so excited about this technology, they decided to keep the invention 'Top Secret'.

At this time, the Allies were winning the World War, so the Navy didn't use the technology after all, and they only allowed it to be seen by the public forty years later in the 1980's. Hedy's invention then became of great interest to some of the biggest computer companies in the world.

Over the next twenty years, top scientists and engineers would experiment and develop Hedy's invention. They would try and use this type of communication with lots of different types of machines. It was when some scientists combined the internet together with Hedy's idea that her invention changed the world. From Hedy's 'frequency hopping' idea, the technology was created that allows mobile phones to communicate and for Wi-Fi to work. The next time that you send emojis to your friends, watch your favourite movie on Netflix, Skype your family or play Pokemon Go - Hedy is one of the people you need to thank!

In the next few years, thanks to Hedy's invention and the hard work of thousands of scientists and engineers, we are going to see some fascinating new inventions and changes to the way we live. Cars will drive themselves, you'll be able to switch off machines with your phone - and fridges will even be able to order shopping so that you'll never run out of your favourite ice cream again. I can't wait - I wonder what Hedy would have thought?

Chapter 4: Rosa Parks

In the Deep South of the United States of America, the weather is hot and sultry. The majestic Mississippi river winds its way slowly through the lush, tropical landscape, covered with cotton and sugar plantations.

It was also a place where people did not live happily together. When people originally came to build their plantations – they brought people from Africa to work for them. The people from Africa had not chosen to come, but were captured and brought to work as slaves. For hundreds of years, these people were treated terribly. They weren't even allowed to pick their names, were separated from their families and had no freedom to do even the simplest things that you and I take for granted.

In 1861, the North of the United States of America went to war with the Southern states over this terrible way of living (called the American Civil War). The North won. This meant that millions of people who were kept as slaves were freed. Sadly, the lack of fairness in life continued in the

Southern states. African-Americans were not allowed to vote unless they took special tests, they weren't allowed to go to the same schools as white children and they weren't even allowed to use the same drinking fountains as white people, simply because they had a different skin colour. And this is where the story of Rosa Parks begins.

Rosa was born fifty years after the end of the American Civil War and grew up in Alabama, one of the Southern States of America. Her Grandfather and Grandmother had been slaves and still talked of those terrible times. Rosa was brought up to believe in what was fair and to stick up for herself. She was a poorly child and was small for her age. She suffered from terrible tonsillitis for the first years of her life and because there were no antibiotics, you can probably imagine how sick she got!

But even when she was little, she knew that life was different for her because she was black. When she started to go to school at six years old, she was aware that not only were children separated based on their skin colour, but that her primary school was small and crowded. Her school had been built by parents, it didn't have heating and up to sixty children were taught in just one room. However, the school for the white children was completely different - it had been built by the local government and was big and clean and warm.

Rosa grew up, trained to be a teacher and met her husband-to-be Raymond. They got married and settled down in Montgomery, Alabama, where she worked as a seamstress. At this time, African-Americans were getting more and more frustrated with the laws that kept people separate. It was impossible to be treated fairly and feel safe in the towns and cities where they lived, but they knew that disobeying these laws could be met with prison or force.

One day, Rosa was getting a bus into town to go to work. There were separate seats on the bus for black people and separate seats for white people. There was a rule that if a white person got on the bus and there were no seats, a black person had to get up and offer their seat. It was one of those busy days and Rosa was sitting down after a hard day at work. A white man got on and the bus driver yelled to Rosa to give up her seat. She didn't. The bus driver yelled at her again, and all the people on the bus were looking at her. Again she didn't move. Rosa said later, she "had no idea that history was being made. I was just tired of giving up".

Because she refused to offer her seat, Rosa was arrested and taken to a busy, smelly jail in the heart of the city. Shortly after, she was taken to court and found guilty of civil disobedience. She didn't get sent to prison, but was fined $14 (which is worth about £100 today).

It was this small act that changed history in America. Rosa hadn't hurt anyone and she hadn't made a big speech. She had simply decided to take one small action. Admittedly, it was a brave decision, but she believed that "you must never be fearful about what you are doing when it is right".

This was the moment that people needed. African-American people across the city joined together and decided to make a stand. They decided to make their feelings very clear about the unfair rules by refusing to take the buses. This caused big problems for the bus companies, as they needed to make money by having passengers. It sent a big message to the people who made money that it was important to treat all their passengers well and it was a great example of what can be achieved if you work together.

You may be wondering how people still earned money and managed to go to work if they didn't use the buses? A very clever and simple taxi system was set up, so that people could still keep working but not a pay a penny to the bus companies who thought it was OK to separate people based on skin colour.

At the same time, peaceful resistance to unfair laws was starting to take hold across the Southern states. Within a year, the laws that separated people on public transport were banned, but there was still a great deal of work to be done to end the poor treatment of people based on skin colour in America. It was a huge achievement to change the laws, but it can take time to change what people believe and how they behave.

Rosa Parks became the symbol of strength and dignity for equal rights for people of all colours and the starting point for this to happen. She is now known as the 'mother of the civil rights movement'. Not because she was famous, not because she was incredibly clever – but because she had the courage to take a small, peaceful action and stand up for what was right.

Chapter 5: Anne Frank

Anne Frank came from a close, happy family. She lived in Amsterdam, Netherlands with her dad, Otto, her mum, Edith and her sister Margot. She had glossy black hair, bright shining eyes and a smile that made everyone feel at ease. At fourteen years old, she was great fun to be with and very popular. She wasn't the cleverest girl at school but did fine in all her subjects – when she tried! She was known as Mrs Chatterbox and loved going out to parties, ice skating and Hollywood movies. This probably sounds like you or your friends at school. The big difference was that Anne Frank was Jewish and she lived in the Netherlands, when the German army invaded the country in 1940.

At this time, Adolf Hitler was the leader of the Nazi Party and ruled Germany. This party hated Jewish people, and other types of people. The Nazis believed that the Jews had no right to live in ordinary society and that everything should be done to get rid of them. When the Nazis started to rule the Netherlands (just as they had done in the other countries that they had invaded) they started to impose terrible laws and rules that picked on Jewish people because of their religion. This was naturally a very worrying time for Anne, her family and all her friends. Slowly but surely the way they lived was starting to change for the worse.

The first thing that changed was at school. One day, Anne and her Jewish friends were taken into a room and told by the teacher that they would not be allowed to come back. A new law had been passed that meant that Jewish children were not allowed to be taught in the same schools as other children. As you can imagine, this really upset Anne and Margot. Slowly but surely, they were stopped from doing all the things they loved. They weren't allowed to go to ice rinks or sports grounds, they had to wear badges at all times that showed they were Jewish and rumours were starting that the Germans were ordering Jewish people to go to work camps where they were treated terribly.

Anne's dad, Otto, was incredibly worried about this and started to make some plans. He ran a business in a beautiful, tall building beside one of the prettiest canals in Amsterdam. On the ground floor was a warehouse where the goods he bought and sold were kept. On the first floor, up a huge sweeping staircase, were the offices where people worked. On the next floor, high, high up was a small part of the building, that not many people could see or knew was there. It was known as the 'annexe'. Otto hatched a daring plan. Just in case life was going to get more difficult and dangerous for Jewish people, Otto decided to clear up this annexe and turn it into a hiding place for his family and friends. He built a secret door – that could only be found behind a bookcase by clicking a special lock.

Then, one afternoon, a letter arrived for the family. The Germans wanted them all to report to a special location the very next morning. Thousands of other Jewish people in the country had received this letter. Otto knew that this was very bad news. His plan that he thought might only be a possibility, was now becoming real. That afternoon they broke the news to Anne and Margot that they were to go into hiding the very next morning. Naturally the girls were scared, sad and very shocked that their lives would change in this way.

Early the next morning, they sneaked into the annexe – along with four other people. It was a small space and they weren't allowed to make any noise in the day, for fear that the people who worked in the office would hear them. The annexe had four small rooms that served as bedrooms and a living room. Anne mentioned in her diary that this was seen as 'luxurious' for a hiding space, but still – to live there day in, day out and never feel the wind in her hair or to be able to run through grass for two years, must have been really terrible and difficult. They couldn't use the toilet during the day and had only a small tin bath with nowhere private to wash in.

This is where Anne started her diary. Her diary, whom she called 'Kitty' was the book which kept all her thoughts and details of what life in the annexe. As you can imagine, living in a small space, with little food and lots of people was very difficult. People got cross, tired and scared and never were able to go outside. Nevertheless, they managed to stay hidden.

There were only three people who knew that the annexe was being used as a hiding place. These were the only people who could get food and supplies for the hidden families. Sometimes it was really difficult to sneak extra food without someone finding out or becoming suspicious, so the families often were hungry or didn't have much food to choose from. Throughout this time, Anne kept as cheery as she could. She invented games, wrote, still took lessons from the other people in the annexe and tried to make the very best of an incredibly difficult situation. She was brave, kept herself strong and always tried to find the joy in the trickiest of things.

One day, she heard on the radio that people were asking for diaries and any written documents to be kept, so that no one could forget how difficult life in the war had been and how terrible it was to hate people because of their religion, skin colour or differences. Anne was hopeful and excited that her diary could be used to help make sure that future generations would never forget this terrible time.

Anne had been hiding with her family for two years in the small annexe, and the Nazis were starting to lose the war. Everyone hiding in the anexe was hopeful that they could survive and emerge safe and sound. Then, one terrible day, the German police arrived at the office demanding to know where the hidden people were. The people who knew that Anne and her family were in the annexe had no choice but to tell the Germans.

The families were rounded up. Anne and her family were put on a train with no food and little water and made to stand and sleep in a crowded space for three days. They arrived at a camp called Auschwitz, which the Nazis had built specifically to round up and get rid of Jewish people and other people that they disliked. The men were separated from the women. Anne, Margot and their mum survived in the cold, with little food, few clothes and made to work all the hours of the day.

Anne and Margot became ill and were separated from their mother and moved to a different camp. They were treated even worse at that camp and became even more ill. Throughout this time, Anne and her sister did everything they could to take care of each other, but their bodies were getting weaker and weaker. Anne and Margot caught a really bad illness and died, only weeks before the Germans lost the war and the people from the camps were freed. Six million Jewish people were killed by the Nazis in the War, which is almost the same number of people who live in London today.

Anne's father was the only person from the family who managed to survive. When he returned to Amsterdam, the news that he had lost his family broke his heart. It was then that he was given Anne's diary. The office workers had found it after the families had been discovered, but had left it unopened. When he read it, he understood that his daughter's diary explained perfectly how terrible war and discrimination are. He made it his life's purpose to make sure that as many people as possible read her diary and understood.

Anne Frank's diary is one of the most famous diaries in the whole world. Her writing has helped make sure that people never forget what happened in World War 2, and through remembering, help stop something as terrible as this ever happening again.

Chapter 6: Martha Payne

There is a small town called Lochgilphead on the west coast of Scotland, where the Scottish Highlands start and the air is fresh and clear. It's not a place that is famous for any particular reason - in fact, lots of people have probably never heard of it.

In 2012, Martha Payne was nine years old and went to the local primary school in Lochgilphead. It was a small school and nothing very exciting ever happened there. Martha and her friends did not like their school lunches – they did not find them healthy, tasty or even filling. Sadly, the adults didn't really listen to them. (Most grown-ups remember their school dinners being pretty yucky too.) But Martha decided to do something. She wanted adults to understand what the children were eating for lunch and why they were complaining. With the help of her Dad, she launched a blog, called 'Never Seconds'.

On this blog, she took photos of every school lunch

she was served and gave it a restaurant style review and rating. Her very first review was posted in May 2012. The photo was of a single pizza slice, a potato croquette, a sprinkle of sweetcorn and a cupcake. It looked boring, it looked unhealthy and it certainly didn't look enough to fill anyone's tummy. The readers of her blog were shocked at what they saw and shared it with other people. They in turn, shared it with others and very quickly, Martha's blog became big news.

In the next couple of weeks, Martha's blog had started to gain the attention of newspapers, celebrities and politicians across the UK. Within one month, there had been three million visits to her blog some from as far away as Taiwan and Germany. Kids across the world were excited about Martha's blog and started to upload their own school dinners and share their pictures with the website. Martha was amazed and delighted by the attention the blog was getting and decided to put it to good use, by asking people to donate money to Mary's Meals, a charity which funds school meals for children in Malawi.

On the 14th June, just one month after Martha had started her blog, she was called out of her maths class and taken to the Head Teacher's office. The local politicians were not happy that their school meals were attracting so much attention. Rather than try to improve the school meals, they tried to stop Martha from publishing more photos and comments. Martha obeyed and her Dad put up a final story on the website letting people know that she had been asked to stop blogging.

But the people who followed the blog were watching. People thought that it was unreasonable and unfair for a local council to try and silence a young girl. Everyone should have the right to speak up about things that they disagree with. Newspapers, TV, radio, politicians and famous people made a big fuss about the fact that Martha had been stopped from blogging and the story quickly made news across the UK and beyond. Because Martha had so many people supporting her, the local council backed down and allowed her to continue writing. As a result of this attention, donations to the charity got bigger and bigger – until they reached £63,000 on the day that Martha was allowed to start her reviews again. They say that 'every cloud has a silver lining' and in this case it certainly did.

In two years, Martha became one of the most famous schoolgirls in the UK. What's more, a great deal of good came out of her simple blog. Not only did the school meals at Martha's school improve, but her website started a discussion across the world about making school dinners healthier and tastier for children. What's more, over £145,000 was raised to help children in Malawi have better meals and a better, healthier start in life.

Martha has won several awards for her fundraising and hard work, has written a book and talks at important events. In 2014, after two years, Martha stopped writing her blog – but you can still find it at www.neverseconds.blogspot.co.uk'.

Thank you so much for reading.

Please leave me a review on Amazon, I'd love to hear what you thought of the book. If there are any other girls and women you would like me to write about for the next book, please leave these suggestions too!

Bibliography & Further Reading

Yousafzai, Malala, and Patricia McCormick. *I Am Malala*. 1st ed. Print.

Lovelace, Ada King, and Betty Alexandra Toole. *Ada, The Enchantress Of Numbers*. Mill Valley, Calif.: Strawberry Press, 1998. Print.

Rhodes, Richard. *Hedy's Folly*. New York: Vintage Books, 2013. Print.

Robbins, Trina, Cynthia Martin, and Anne Timmons. *Hedy Lamarr And A Secret Communication System*. Mankato, Minn.: Capstone Press, 2007. Print.

Parks, Rosa, and James Haskins. *Rosa Parks*. 1st ed. [Bridgewater, NJ]: Distributed by Paw Prints/Baker & Taylor, 2009. Print.

Frank, Anne, B. M Mooyaart-Doubleday, and Storm Jameson. *Anne Frank's Diary*. London: Vallentine, Mitchell, 1987. Print.

Lee, Carol Ann. *Anne Frank's Story*. 1st ed.
[Mahwah, N.J.]: Troll, 2002. Print.

Payne, Martha, and Dave Payne. *Neverseconds*. 1st
ed. Glasgow: Cargo, 2012. Print.

About Girlguiding

Girlguiding is the leading charity for girls and
young women in the UK. It builds girls' confidence
and raises their aspirations. It gives them the
chance to discover their full potential and
encourage them to be a powerful force for good. It
gives them a space to have fun. Girls and
volunteers in Girlguiding join a worldwide family of
over ten million people in 146 countries, aged
from five years old upwards.

If you are interested in joining Girlguiding, or
volunteering, please visit www.girlguiding.org.uk.

22190037R00032

Printed in Great Britain
by Amazon